LIBRARIANS

by Meg Gaertner

Cody Koala
An Imprint of Pop!
popbooksonline.com

abdopublishing.com
Published by Pop!, a division of ABDO, PO Box 398166, Minneapolis,
Minnesota 55439. Copyright © 2019 by POP, LLC. International copyrights
reserved in all countries. No part of this book may be reproduced in any
form without written permission from the publisher. Pop!™ is a trademark
and logo of POP, LLC.

Printed in the United States of America, North Mankato, Minnesota

042018
092018

THIS BOOK CONTAINS
RECYCLED MATERIALS

Cover Photo: Shutterstock Images
Interior Photos: Shutterstock Images, 1, 9 (bottom right), 15, 16 (top),
16 (middle), 16 (bottom), 20; iStockphoto, 5, 6, 9 (top), 9 (bottom left), 11, 12, 19
(top), 19 (bottom left), 19 (bottom right)

Editor: Charly Haley
Series Designer: Laura Mitchell

Library of Congress Control Number: 2017963377

Publisher's Cataloging-in-Publication Data
Names: Gaertner, Meg, author.
Title: Librarians / by Meg Gaertner.
Description: Minneapolis, Minnesota : Pop!, 2019. | Series: Community
   workers | Includes online resources and index.
Identifiers: ISBN 9781532160127 (lib.bdg.) | ISBN 9781532161247 (ebook) |
Subjects: LCSH: Librarians--Juvenile literature. | Libraries and community-
   -Juvenile literature. | Library employees--Juvenile literature. |
   Occupations--Careers--Jobs--Juvenile literature. | Community life--
   Juvenile literature.
Classification: DDC 020.9--dc23

Hello! My name is
Cody Koala

Pop open this book and you'll find QR codes like this one, loaded with information, so you can learn even more!

Scan this code* and others like it while you read, or visit the website below to make this book pop.

popbooksonline.com/librarians

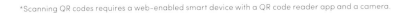

*Scanning QR codes requires a web-enabled smart device with a QR code reader app and a camera.

Table of Contents

Chapter 1

A Day in the Life

A boy walks into the **library**.

He wants a book about

animals. He knows the

librarian can help him find it.

Watch a video here!

The librarian leads the

boy through rows of books.

The librarian suggests
many books about animals.
The boy checks out books to
take home to read.

There are more than
119,000 libraries in
the United States.

Chapter 2

The Work

Librarians **organize** information so people can find it easily. They organize books in libraries.

Learn more here!

People can also use computers, newspapers, and movies to find information at libraries. Librarians organize this information.

The Library of Congress in Washington, DC, is home to more than 164 million items!

Librarians help people understand technology. They teach people how to use computers to find information.

Most librarians work in libraries and schools.

Chapter 3

Tools for Librarians

Librarians use **catalogs** on the computer. These catalogs have notes on every book in the library. People can look up books by writer or by topic.

Learn more here!

barcode scanner

This scans books so librarians can keep track of them.

book cart

library card

People need a library card to check out books.

Librarians check out books with a **scanner**. They scan the person's library card and the books that the person wants. This helps librarians know who has each book.

Chapter 4

Helping the Community

Librarians create a safe space that welcomes everyone. They organize fun learning events for the community. Anyone can use a library.

Complete an activity here!

Librarians are here to answer any question. If they do not know the answer, they will find it for you or help you find it for yourself.

Making Connections

Text-to-Self

Have you ever met a librarian? What did you think of him or her? Would you ever want to be a librarian?

Text-to-Text

Have you read other books about community workers? How are their jobs different from a librarian's?

Text-to-World

Why is it important that everyone has access to information at the library?

Glossary

catalog – an organized list of every item in a library.

library – a place that keeps books, newspapers, and other forms of information that everyone can use.

organize – to put things in a neat and clear order.

scanner – a machine that scans something and turns it into information on a computer.

Index

Online Resources

popbooksonline.com

Thanks for reading this Cody Koala book!

Scan this code* and others like it in this book, or visit the website below to make this book pop!

popbooksonline.com/librarians

*Scanning QR codes requires a web-enabled smart device with a QR code reader app and a camera.